MIRRA IMAGES

TRANNY-TO-TRANNY TAILWHIP AT MY NEW TRAINING FACILITY.
RIDING AT THE WAREHOUSE IS ROUNDING OUT MY SKILLS FOR SURE.

MIRRA IMAGES

DAVE MIRRA THE STORY OF MY LIFE

WITH MARK LOSEY

ReganBooks
An Imprint of HarperCollinsPublishers

HarperCollins books may be purchased for educational, business, or sales promotional use. For information please write: Special Markets Department, HarperCollins Publishers Inc., 10 East 53rd Street, New York, NY 10022.

FIRST EDITION

Designed by P.R. Brown @ Bau-Da Design Lab

Library of Congress Cataloging-in-Publication Data

Mirra, Dave, 1974–
Mirra images : the story of my life / Dave Mirra with Mark Losey. -- 1st ed
p. cm.
ISBN 0-06-098916-5
1. Mirra, Dave, 1974–2. Cyclists--United States--Biography. 3. Bicycle motocross.
I. Losey, Mark. II. Title.

GV1051.M57A3 2003
796.6'2'092--dc21
[B]

2003047207

03 04 05 06 07 QNM/QW 10 9 8 7 6 5 4 3 2 1

For my mom and dad

I DEBUTED MY VERSION OF THE CARVING FLAIR AT THE 2001 ANAHEIM B3 CONTEST. I GUESS THE JUDGES LIKED IT, SINCE IT HELPED ME WIN THE COMP

CONTENTS

ONE HAPPY TEN-YEAR-OLD. SEE THAT CURVED FRAME IN THE BACKGROUND? THAT'S WHY I'M LAUGHING.

It all started when my brother, Tim, who was two years older, gave me a red hand-me-down bike when I was about three years old. It was too big for me, and since I was so small, I had to use the curb in front of my house as a ladder to get onboard. (I could reach the pedals, just not the ground.) There were no training wheels attached to the bike, which meant I spent more time lying on the ground than anything else, but I was determined to learn how to ride. My neighbor and babysitter Karen Ralston was watching me struggle to keep my bike upright and decided to give me a hand. She pushed me down the street and somehow it all clicked in my head—I finally figured out how to balance. To Karen I must have looked like just another wobbly kid learning to ride, but for me, it was the start of big things.

INTRODUCTION

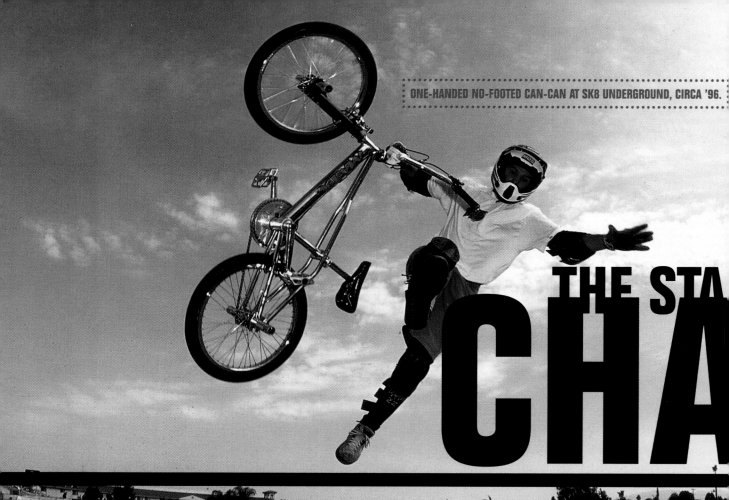

THE STA
CHA

OF BIG THINGS
PTER 1

THE START OF BIG THINGS

CHAPTER 1

I was born on April 4, 1974, in Chittenango, New York, a small town about twenty miles west of Syracuse. My parents divorced when I was four and my brother, Tim, and I stayed with my dad in Chittenango, while my mom moved to Syracuse. Even though we didn't live with her, I saw her every weekend, and she and I were really close.

Although Tim was older, he was one of my best friends. We had plenty of brotherly "disagreements," but even when we argued, we still rode our bikes together for hours every day. By the time I was nine, we were completely hooked on riding and spent our free time pedaling around the neighborhood and jumping off curbs. Eventually, Shawn Wagner joined us. He was my age and lived right down the street. Through him, we were introduced to a new type of bike riding—BMX freestyle (even though at the time we didn't know it had a name).

Shawn's older brother, Gene, was in high school, and he and his friends did tricks on their bikes that Tim and I had never seen. The first time I saw them ride, one of the guys jumped his bike in the air, spun 180 degrees, and landed going backward—all without a ramp! I was blown away and studied every move they made so I could learn to ride the same way.

But it didn't end with bike tricks; Gene and his friends also raced BMX, in which eight riders went through dirt berms and jumps to see who could cross the finish line first. Tim and I both thought racing looked cool and we had everything we needed for the track—a twenty-inch bike and a helmet. The nearest BMX track was forty-five minutes away in Liverpool, New York. With our parents' busy work schedules, getting to the track on a weekly basis was next to impossible, so after two races my BMX racing "career" was over.

Since we couldn't make it to the BMX track, Tim and I had to get creative. We started riding everything possible. We made ramps and jumped over garbage cans, or had wheelie contests to see who could go the farthest—we did anything we could think of as long as it kept us on our bikes. We were on the same level trickwise, so we could learn the same tricks and push each other to do better.

BIRTHDAY NUMBER THREE. THE FLAT BILL ON MY HAT IS THE BEST PART OF THE PICTURE.

ME AND MY BRO, WINTER 1981.

Pedal stand on my Diamondback Silver Streak in the fall of 1985. The only two things I needed at this point were back brakes and a haircut.

ICEPICK ON THE RAIL AT JAYCEE SKATEPARK IN 1996. NOT MANY PEOPLE WERE USING RAILS ON THE BACK OF RAMPS AT THAT POINT.

CH

FREESTYLE

In 1984, while Tim and I were visiting our mom, my step-dad ran across a story in the paper about a bike show that was going on in Liverpool. He didn't know exactly what type of show it was, but he knew that as long as it involved bikes, Tim and I would be into it.

When we got to the show, my brother and I were amazed. A bike company named Haro sent a team of professional riders on tour every year to do demos on portable ramps and on flatland, and that's what this show was all about. That year, the team consisted of Rich Sigur and Ron Wilton, who were two of the top pros at the time, and Bob Haro, a rider who was credited in the 1970s with pioneering the sport of "BMX freestyle," meaning any trick done on a BMX bike. He also founded Haro Bicycles, which is still one of the most popular companies in the sport.

CHAPTER 2
FREESTYLE EQUALS MY STYLE

Seeing the Haro team in person put bike riding in a new perspective—*this* was freestyle. Tim and I were already doing some of the tricks we saw in the show, but we never made the connection that it was an actual *sport* until that day. At the time there were no major BMX events like the X Games on television, so seeing the traveling demos was the only way to see pro-level riding.

As soon as we got home, we immediately started trying to learn the tricks we saw in the show. We didn't have any ramps, so we worked on ground-based, flatland tricks instead. Learning them became an addiction; I couldn't get enough.

By junior high school, bike riding had become a huge part of my life, but it wasn't the only sport I was into. Tim and I took tennis lessons for a year and played a lot of golf, which is something I still do today. I also played on a community basketball league for three years, which was awesome. It got to the point where I was scoring forty points a game before the coach would pull me out for hogging the ball. Still, I never stopped riding my bike. There were times when I slacked off, but it wouldn't be long until I was right back out in the street learning new tricks.

When it came to school, I did what I had to do to pass and that was about it. During sixth-grade social studies I'd stare at BMX magazines all day instead of paying attention, and my teacher, Mr. Jackson, always gave me a hard time. He would say things like, "Dave, you're not going anywhere on that bike. If you ever get a picture in a magazine, I'll apologize to you." I was a cocky kid, so I usually picked up the magazine, pointed at a photo, and said, "See these guys? They make way more than you do!" I may have been too wise for my own good, but there was no way I was going to let him knock bike riding and get away with it. My parents could tell how important bike riding was to me, so they never really pressured me to work harder in school. I was never a terrible student, but at the same time, the As were not exactly flying my way.

SIXTH-GRADE POWER MOWER ON MY HARO MASTER.
CHECK THE COMB IN THE BACK POCKET—STYLE.

JUST ANOTHER AFTER-SCHOOL SESSION IN THE BASEMENT. DON'T TELL MY DAD.

THE FIVE RIDERS WHO INFLUENCED ME THE MOST

1. DENNIS MCCOY. I grew up watching Dennis ride both vert and flatland at a top level. Dennis was the leader of the new school in the late eighties, and his style of riding put him in his own class. When I was growing up, I wanted to ride just like him.

2. RON WILKERSON. At one time Ron was the hottest rider in the sport. He was a trendsetter with his clothes and the style of his riding. Ron was the first rider to do advanced lip tricks on a quarterpipe, and he invented one of the most popular street tricks today, the abubaca. Ron brought a skate influence to BMX when he started the 2-Hip contest series in the late eighties. He helped make a change in BMX attire from leathers and jerseys to shorts and T-shirts.

3. MIKE DOMINGUEZ. I've always looked up to Mike for his huge riding style—he made it look effortless. When Mike rode, anyone could tell it was pure talent.

4. MARK EATON. When I was fourteen years old, I was really into flatland. Mark was one of the best amateurs in the sport and very respected for his originality. I met Mark at a small contest in Pennsylvania, and he invited me to come ride with the infamous Plywood Hoods. Mark also produced a video called *Dorkin' in York,* and when *Dorkin' 2* came out, I had a section in the video.

5. MAT HOFFMAN. I started getting more into ramp riding in 1988, and Mat was pushing the riding limits every day, coming up with tricks that had never been done. Mat dominated for years, and in the early nineties he introduced the backflip fakie on vert. Watching Mat ride gave me inspiration and motivation to take my riding to the next level.

WE HAD TO SHOVEL SNOW TO RIDE RON SMITH'S RAMP DURING THE WINTER, AND HALF THE TIME WE HAD TO WAIT UNTIL IT WAS BELOW FREEZING SO THE RAMP WOULD STAY DRY.

FREESTYLE EQUALS MY STYLE

BIG 540 AT RON SMITH'S RAMP IN THE WINTER OF 1991. THAT WHITE STUFF ON THE GROUND HAD A LOT TO DO WITH MY LEAVING NEW YORK.

CHAP

EIGHTEEN-FOOT RAMP, NINETEEN-FOOT AIR AT THE DC SUPER RAMP.

EIGHTEEN-FOOT RAMP, NINETEEN-FOOT AIR
AT THE DC SUPER RAMP.

SPONSORS, CONTESTS, AND THE

SPONSORS, CONTESTS, AND THE PLYWOOD HOODS

CHAPTER 3

By 1987, freestyle had gotten so popular that there were a lot of demo teams traveling around the country. For aspiring riders, going to the bike shows was a great way to meet the pros and learn new tricks. That year in April, the General Bikes team came to Lindy's Bike Loft in North Syracuse to do a show, and I made sure to be there. Before the show started I was riding flatland in the bike store's parking lot when one of the General pros, Fred Blood, noticed my riding. Even though I was only thirteen, I was pretty advanced at flatland and was pulling double decades (which are done by pulling the front end of the bike off the ground and then jumping over the front end twice while the front wheel is still off the ground). Not too many riders in the country were pulling that trick off at the time, so Fred was pretty surprised to see me, a five-foot-tall kid from Chittenango, pull one.

Fred went into the shop and told the owners, Marianne and Lance Lindy, about me. They sponsored a local freestyle team that did demos around town, and Fred told them that they had to put me on it.

Later that day Fred introduced me to Marianne and Lance and helped me work out my first sponsorship deal: discounts on the parts sold in the shop in exchange for riding in the team's shows. This was a huge deal because at the time, every penny I could get ahold of went to buy bike parts. General also agreed to cosponsor me, which meant I got a discount on a General bike that was way too big for me. But the size of the bike didn't matter—I was now sponsored. That summer, Lindy's held tryouts for new team riders, and Tim and my cousin Jamie both made the team as well.

RAMP ACCESS

As a Lindy team member, I got to ride to the team's portable quarterpipe during weekly practice sessions at the shop. I became friends with the other riders on the team, including Mark Lamorie, who at sixteen years of age happened to be the owner of a sixteen-foot-wide, eight-foot-tall half-pipe that he and his friends had built in his backyard. I had never even been near a halfpipe that big before, and suddenly he was inviting me to ride it whenever I wanted. The only problem was that getting to his house was a bit of an ordeal, since he lived twenty-five miles away in North Syracuse. Once a week Tim, Jamie, and I would ride our bikes two and a half hours to get there. When we finally showed up, we would stay for the weekend and ride nonstop.

Riding the halfpipe was a lot different than riding Lindy's quarterpipe. On the halfpipe, to gain momentum I had to use my arms and legs to pump as I went up and down each side to keep going higher. It seemed like forever before I got it down, but the more I rode, the more comfortable I got. I learned to go a foot or two out of the top of the ramp, and the day I finally broke three feet everything fell into place. I started going higher while doing tricks at the same time, and it wasn't long before I could ride the ramp better than everyone on the team.

MY EARLY QUARTERPIPE SKILLS IN

MIBRA IMAGES

87

HELLO, TEAM HARO

In August, I went to Wayne's Bike Shop in Liverpool—where I'd seen my first freestyle show ever—to see the latest installment of Haro's freestyle show. The riders in the show consisted of Brian Blyther, Ron Wilkerson, and Dave Nourie, three top pros I had met at a show the year before. Again, I was riding flatland in the parking lot while waiting for the team to show up, and just as they pulled in I pulled another double decade. They got out of the van yelling, "I can't believe you just did that! That was amazing!"

Once the Haro show ended, I hung out with the team and told them how I had gotten cosponsored by General four months earlier. I was fully stoked on the General deal, but then Bill Hawkins, Haro's team manager, offered me a better cosponsorship deal with Haro—complete with a free bike of my choice and the promise that if I went to a major competition, Haro would pay for my food and lodging! I was on cloud nine.

CONTEST NUMBER ONE

Once on the Haro team, I couldn't wait to enter a big freestyle contest, so two months later I asked my dad to drive me to Columbus, Ohio, for the American Freestyle Association's (AFA) Masters Series. The AFA contests were held in different cities around the country, and this was the closest one had come to my house since I'd gotten sponsored by Haro. I met up with the Haro guys when I got to Columbus, and I couldn't believe how they took me in. My dad even got his own hotel room so I could stay with the Haro guys and hang out with the rest of the team.

The following day, when the contest started, I was so nervous and excited that I was about to explode. I entered the 13 and Under Expert Flatland class, but during my sixty-second routine anxiety got the best of me, and I fell apart. I didn't pull a lot of my tricks, which left me in eleventh place out of twelve riders, but I wasn't too upset because I still had a great time. A lot of kids my age were into collecting the pros' autographs, but I was riding and learning tricks right along with them.

The Columbus contest was also where I met Dennis McCoy, one of the premier BMX freestyle riders and a major hero of mine. Dennis rode ramps and flatland, and his flatland style was so progressive that everyone was playing catch-up. Just getting to meet and ride with Dennis made the trip to Ohio worth it.

In 1988, the freestyle industry as a whole was starting to feel financial hard times. Freestyle bike sales had tapered off and riders were getting dropped from teams left and right. Eventually even Haro was forced to

MY "CALIFORNIA LOOK" IN 1990. ME HANGING WITH MY MOM.

make budget cutbacks, and that translated into my getting dropped from the team. I was bummed to lose my ride, but I didn't let it stop me. My parents were still supersupportive, and my dad drove Tim and me to contests all over the Northeast.

THE PLYWOOD HOODS

That summer, I went to Bristol, Pennsylvania—a little more than 300 miles from home—for a contest hosted by Charlie's Bike Shop. I rode well and won my flatland and quarterpipe classes, but more important, I met Kevin Jones, Mark Eaton, and Brett Downs, three riders from York, Pennsylvania, who were part of a team called the Plywood Hoods. The Hoods were legendary because their flatland riding had completely changed the face of freestyle, and they were constantly getting coverage in the BMX magazines. Before the Hoods, flatland revolved around stationary balance and hopping tricks, but the Hoods were inventing tricks that were performed while their bikes rolled forward, or they kicked the tire with their foot to "scuff" forward or backward. Sometimes the Hoods didn't do the best in contests, but their tricks were so groundbreaking that everyone in freestyle was dying to see them ride.

While I was at the contest in Bristol, the Hoods invited me to York to ride with them. All I had to do was figure out my transportation. Another contest was going to take place in Wayne, New Jersey, the next week, so my dad drove me there. When it ended, I caught a ride with Mark Eaton and his crew to York, which was 280 miles away. The plan was for me to stay with them for a week, at the end of which we would all travel to a contest in Albany, New York, and Eaton would drop me back off in Chittenango on his way home.

The Hoods were all older than I was and some of them had regular jobs, but while I was in York, all I wanted to do was ride all day, every day. I was wide awake by 6:30 every morning, and I would wake up anyone I was staying with by yelling, "Come on, let's ride!" The Hoods may have been a little annoyed, but someone was always down to ride.

In 1987, the Hoods had also started making their own freestyle videos, which were creating huge waves in the sport. A few lame how-to videos were out, but the Hoods' *Dorkin' in York,* was the real deal. Incredible riding, good music, a great vibe—it was just what riders were dying to see. While I was in York, Eaton managed to get enough flatland and ramp footage of me to include in *Dorkin' 2.* It was my first video part ever, and I was only fourteen years old.

MARK LAMORIE, RON SMITH, AND ME TAKING A BREAK ON A HOT SUMMER DAY.

MY FIVE FAVORITE MOVIES

1. *BEAUTIFUL GIRLS*
2. *CADDYSHACK*
3. *ROUNDERS*
4. *SCHINDLER'S LIST*
5. *ROCKY IV*

SPONSORS, CONTESTS, AND THE PLYWOOD HOODS

THE TURNAROUGH

TALL NO-HANDER ON WOODWARD'S OUTDOOR
VERT RAMP IN 1995.

ATTENTION! WARNING!

- HELMET, KNEE PADS, ELBOW PADS,
  AND WRIST GUARDS REQUIRED
  ON THIS RAMP.

- THIS RAMP IS CLOSED UNLESS

APTER 4

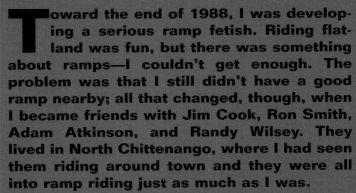

CHAPTER 4
THE TURNAROUND

Toward the end of 1988, I was developing a serious ramp fetish. Riding flatland was fun, but there was something about ramps—I couldn't get enough. The problem was that I still didn't have a good ramp nearby; all that changed, though, when I became friends with Jim Cook, Ron Smith, Adam Atkinson, and Randy Wilsey. They lived in North Chittenango, where I had seen them riding around town and they were all into ramp riding just as much as I was.

There was a dead-end road ten minutes away from my house known to us as the Turnaround. There was rarely any traffic on it, so Jim, Ron, Adam, and Randy used the area to build makeshift ramps out of anything they could find. Sometimes the ramps were nothing more than a couple of boards leaning against a wall, but eventually they figured out how to build an actual quarter-pipe. It was a little rickety compared to the

TOP-SIDE NO-FOOTED CAN-CAN AT MARK LAMORIE'S RAMP IN 1989.

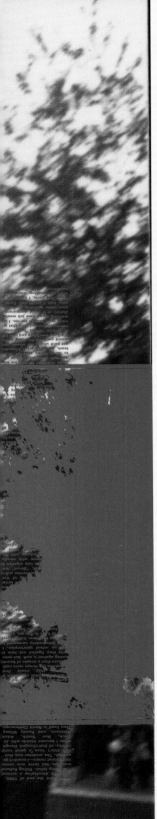

ramps built now, but we were happy to have it. For me, a local ramp turned out to be the ultimate motivator.

The time I put in at The Turnaround and on Mark Lamorie's halfpipe made a big impact on my riding, and I couldn't wait to ride in an actual halfpipe contest. In the summer of 1989, I got my chance. Pro rider Ron Wilkerson was promoting his own halfpipe contest series called the 2-Hip King of Vert along with a street series called Meet the Street. "Street" was first used in the late eighties to describe contests with smaller ramps, grind ledges, and box jumps. It wasn't the same as actually riding ledges and rails on "real street," but it was an easy way to describe what was going on. Street was becoming more and more popular, and street-type contests were starting to blow up.

That summer Ron Smith's dad drove our local crew to a 2-Hip event in central Pennsylvania at Woodward Camp, a training camp/fantasyland for BMX freestyle and racing, skateboarding, and Olympic-style gymnastics. Most of the top amateur and pro ramp riders in the country were in attendance, and since there were no age divisions for amateurs in King of Vert events, I had to compete against riders in their twenties even though I was only fifteen. Still, all of the practice paid off, and I wound up getting eighth out of the twenty-five experts who entered. I was starting to get a reputation as a kid who could have a big future in riding.

That September I went to another 2-Hip event in Long Island, New York, and by then I was really attracting some attention. I was going as high as a lot of the pros and learning new tricks quickly. Dino DeLuca, who was a top pro at the time, was real psyched on the way I was riding and told me that he wanted me on his team. He rode for Dyno and after he told his team manager about me, I got an offer to be a full-on member of the team. As an amateur I wouldn't get paid until I did shows, but I would get paid for every demo I did. I got free bikes and free travel (plane tickets to contests, hotels, and so on), and that was more than enough for me. I was working a part-time job washing dishes at a local restaurant to earn some spending money, but now that I could call Dyno to order free parts, I could see my days of washing dishes were numbered.

CRANKED AND YANKED TURNDOWN
IN MARK LAMORIE'S BARN IN 1988.

TALL SUB BOXES ARE ONE OF MY FAVORITE OBSTACLES TO RIDE. THIS IS AN ICEPICK ON AN EIGHT-FOOTER AT A VANS COMP IN 2001.

CHAPTER
LIFE ON THE ROAD

Getting sponsored by Dyno meant that when the summer of 1990 came around, I would be doing shows at bike shops across the country. Touring was every rider's dream, and I couldn't believe it was happening to me. A month before I went on tour I broke my shoulder doing a 540, but luckily it healed just in time for me to hit the road.

Starting in June, I traveled most of the summer and learned what it's like to sleep in a different hotel every night. Because I was sixteen years old, my parents were a little nervous about me being on the road with a bunch of older riders, but they remained supportive. They knew I loved riding, and they wanted me to succeed.

R5

CHAPTER 5
LIFE ON THE ROAD

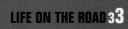

SUMMER POSE RIGHT BEFORE GRADUATION.

When the tour ended in August, I figured I should go back to my normal life, which meant going back to work. I returned to the restaurant to wash dishes, but that only lasted for a few weeks before I decided I'd had enough. I had saved enough money from the shows to afford to quit and leave the dishes behind.

SAY GOODBYE TO THE GOOD LIFE

In 1991, I graduated high school and decided to get out of Chittenango for a while. I loved traveling and riding, so going to college was never really something I wanted to do. I went back on tour for Dyno, but life on the road had changed a lot from the year before. The duo of Bill Hawkins and Ron Haro—Bob Haro's brother—was now in charge of the Dyno freestyle program, and thanks to lack of money in the freestyle industry, the tour was tough. BMX freestyle companies were trying to stretch every penny, but in our case it was ridiculous. Our truck was overheating all the time, and the company credit card was constantly getting denied. There were even a few times when we had to sit at a gas station for six hours waiting for the credit card's limit to be raised so that we could fix the truck or get gas. I loved riding and being on the road, but this sucked. I couldn't wait for the tour to end.

HELLO, HOFFMAN BIKES

At the end of the tour, I had some time off and could do whatever I wanted. I had some money saved, so I didn't need to stay in Chittenango and work. I had become friends with most of the top riders in the sport from all over the country, and they were like extended family members, so I decided to pay some of them a visit.

That December, Jim Cook and I decided to spend the holidays in the Midwest with some friends. Our first stop was Kansas City, Missouri, to hang out with the KC Rogues—Rick Thorne and Dennis McCoy. Since 1988, when I met Dennis at a contest in Columbus, Ohio, he had become a good friend, and Thorne was a top amateur I had known for years. After Kansas City, Jim and I headed south to spend New Year's Eve with Mat Hoffman—a BMX legend—and his crew in Oklahoma City. Mat had an indoor ramp at his warehouse, and we rode all night and had a blast bringing in the new year.

While I was in Oklahoma, Mat told me that he was about to start an all-new bike company called Hoffman Bikes, and he asked if I would be interested in riding for the team. Riding for Mat sounded awesome, especially since things were so sketchy at Dyno, so I left and became a member of the original Hoffman Bikes team.

SCHOOL SEEMED LIKE IT WOULD NEVER END, SO GRADUATION WAS ONE OF THE BEST DAYS OF MY LIFE.

MIRRA IMAGES

A FRIEND OF MINE NAMED TARRICK RENTED A RUNDOWN
WAREHOUSE IN 1991 AND BUILT A MINI RAMP INSIDE.
ONCE HE GAVE ME A KEY, WINTER WENT BY A LOT FASTER.

DEBUTING THE NEW SUPERMAN-SEATGRAB INDIAN
AIR IN LAKE HAVASU IN 2000.

PRO TIME CHAPTER

CHAPTER 6
PRO TIME

R 6

When Mat launched Hoffman Bikes, he began promoting his own freestyle contests called the Bicycle Stunts (BS) Series. There were no other big contests happening, since freestyle's slowdown was still in effect, so the BS contests became the biggest events of the year. We were a small, tight-knit community, and these contests were the perfect excuse for everyone to get together and have a good time.

The first BS contest was held in Dallas at the beginning of 1992, and that's where I made my pro debut. I was already riding at a pro level on vert ramps and street, so I knew I was ready. There wasn't much money to be won (first place took home four hundred dollars), but calling yourself "pro" was still prestigious. I had a pretty good weekend, getting second place in vert and third in street. Riding against the best pushed me to excel.

Overall, my first year competing as a pro went way better than I expected. At the time, Mat hadn't lost a professional vert contest in three and a half years, but I broke his streak by winning vert at the BS finals that year in Daytona Beach, Florida, and at an international contest called Rider Cup in England. For a rookie, I thought it was a pretty big accomplishment.

THE MIRACLE BOY

Since the freestyle scene was so small in 1992, contests were way more laid back than they are now. The announcers were always other riders, and they usually spent more time telling jokes during riders' runs than calling out the tricks that were being done. That's exactly how I got the "Miracle Boy" nickname. At a contest in Arizona, I was going for some big tricks on vert, like half-barspin-tailwhips, and somehow every trick I tried worked. While I was riding, the two announcers, Steve Swope and Eddie Roman, were freaking out. They were on the microphone yelling, "It's a miracle! He's the miracle boy!" From that day on I was branded the Miracle Boy, whether I liked it or not.

HAVING ACCESS TO TARRICK'S INDOOR MINI RAMP MEANT I COULD SPEND MORE TIME ACTUALLY RIDING RAMPS INSTEAD OF DREAMING ABOUT THEM.

FLIP FLY-OUT AT THE 1992 BS FINALS. I LEARNED FLIPS EARLIER THAT YEAR RIDING A SIXTEEN-INCH BIKE AND USING OLD COUCH CUSHIONS TO SOFTEN THE CRASHES.

...r not.
...was branded The Miracle
...a miracle! He's the mira-
...were freaking out. They were
...the two announcers, Steve
...somehow every trick I tried
...some big tricks on vert, like
...nickname. At a contest in
...were being done. That's exactly
...riders' runs than call-
...other riders, and they usually
...laid back than they are now. The
...scene was so small in 1992,
...I thought it was a pretty big
...contest called Rider Cup
...finals that year in Daytona Beach,
...but I broke his streak by
...Mat hadn't lost a vert
...year competing as a pro went way
...the best pushed me to excel.
...getting second place in vert and
...was still prestigious. I had a
...There wasn't much money
...took home four hundred dollars).
...a pro level on vert ramps and
...that's where I made my pro debut.
...was held in Dallas at the
...a good time.
...the perfect excuse for everyone
...was a small, tight-knit community,
...contests became the biggest
...since freestyle's slowdown was
...BS) Series. There were no other
...freestyle contests called the
...Hoffman Bikes, he began pro-

CHAP

SPROCKET JOCKEYS AND FISTICUFFS
CHAPTER 7

A lot of my year in 1992 was taken up by riding in Sprocket Jockey shows. The Sprocket Jockeys was a demo team run by Mat Hoffman, and we performed all over the United States and Canada on a portable halfpipe and box jump setup. Most of the shows went on for weeks at a time at state fairs, so everyone doing them got a good taste of the carnie lifestyle. Riding at 10 A.M. for six people who were looking for a sideshow attraction wasn't always fun, but it was really the only way to get by as a pro rider—without having to get another job. Plus, riding every day with your friends can never be too bad.

At the beginning of 1993, a Canadian pro named Jay Miron joined the Hoffman team. I had known and ridden with Jay at contests for years, but I had no idea what life on the road or being on the same team with him would be like. In hindsight, I wish I had never found out.

TER 7

Soon after he joined the team, I went on a Sprocket Jockey tour of Canada with Jay, Steve Swope, and Jay's friend Brent Oswald, who was our announcer. Jay and Brent were already tight, and while we were on the tour, Jay and Steve started working out together every day. I wasn't into their workout schedule, so I didn't hang out with them at the gym. Because of this, they did a pretty good job of making me feel like an outsider while we were traveling. Day by day, the tension worsened, and by the end of the trip, I felt like I had been to hell and back—and that was only the beginning.

That fall, Jay, Dennis McCoy, Rick Thorne, and I were in Dallas doing shows at the Texas State Fair. Rain had made the ramps too slippery to ride for one of the performances, so we planned to do a five-minute flatland demo instead. Since it was such a quick show, I was only going to wear jeans and a Sprocket Jockey shirt, but Jay started yelling, "No, you're not, dude! No, you're not!" It seemed like he was trying to be the man in charge, but I wasn't having it, especially since I had been on the team longer than he had. Plus, I thought that Jay had an attitude throughout the trip, so I didn't want to hear anything more from him.

I told Jay that he wasn't in charge of me, and that I was going to wear whatever I wanted. He said, "Why don't you show some responsibility?" I replied with, "Why don't you quit kissing up?" and then a wrestling match broke out. Our fight didn't last very long, but he got a couple of hits in before we got separated.

After the fight, there was no way I was going to do any more shows with Jay. I loaded up my car and drove back to New York, cutting out five days before the end of the fair. To me, it seemed like the right thing to do, but when I went to the BS finals in November, the entire Hoffman Bikes crew gave me the cold shoulder—except for Mat, who was pretty cool about the whole situation. I decided to wear the Hoffman Bikes T-shirt throughout the finals, but by the end of the year I was leaving the HB team.

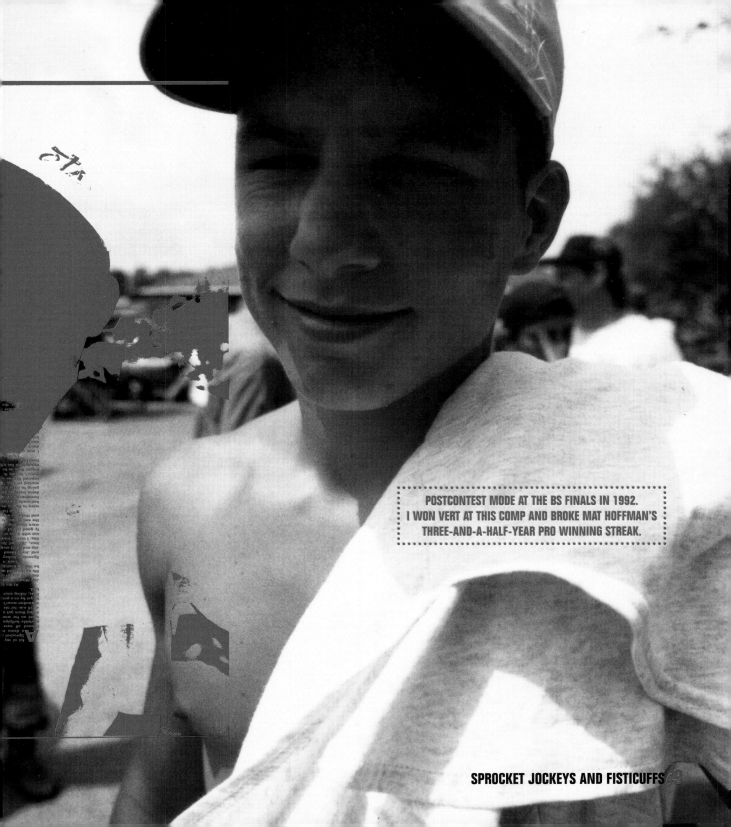

POSTCONTEST MODE AT THE BS FINALS IN 1992.
I WON VERT AT THIS COMP AND BROKE MAT HOFFMAN'S
THREE-AND-A-HALF-YEAR PRO WINNING STREAK.

DOUBLE-BARSPIN DURING ONE OF THE VERY FEW DIRT CONTESTS I EVER ENTERED.

CHA

Once I decided to quit the Hoffman team, I tried to come up with a blueprint for the next year. Woody Itson, GT's freestyle team manager, wanted me to ride for his team. The catch was that I would have to be based in California and go on tour. Both of those requirements were fine with me, so I planned on spending the holidays in New York and then moving to California in January—but I never could have planned for what happened next.

On December 18, 1993, my friends Jim Cook, Frank Taffle, and I were leaving Club Chameleon, an eighteen-and-over club in Syracuse. I bought a piece of pizza at the restaurant next door and started walking across the street when—*bam!* A car going forty-five miles per hour plowed into me. The impact flipped me fifteen feet into the air, and when I finally hit the pavement I was out cold. Jim thought I was dead for sure, but I finally came

DRUNK DRIVERS AND FRACTURED SKULLS
CHAPTER 8

to. I instantly went into shock and started screaming, "Jim, get me out! Get me out!"

To this day I have no recollection of the actual accident. I remember the club and the pizza, but that's where the memory ends. The next thing I knew it was a day and a half later and I woke up from a semi-coma in the intensive care unit. The accident had left me with a fractured skull, a blood clot on my brain, and a severely dislocated shoulder. In all honesty, I was lucky to be alive. I later found out that the girl driving the car that hit me was drunk and not of legal drinking age—quite a mess.

I stayed in the hospital for eight days after the accident, and when I was finally released I had strict instructions not to touch my bike for six months so that the blood clot had time to dissolve. I stayed at my dad's house during my time off and slowly began to regain my strength. There were times when I thought I was fine and ready to ride again, but some severe headaches kept telling me otherwise.

Six months later, I went back to the hospital and was told that the blood clot had finally dissolved. The doctor who examined me was on staff at Syracuse University and told me, "If you played football for Syracuse, I would have to end your career right now because another blow to your head could be fatal. Since you ride a bike, I know I can't do that, but I must warn you that if you hit your head again, you may be in major trouble."

I thanked the doctor for his advice, and a week later my girlfriend and I were in my car on our way to California. Woody still had a spot for me on his team, so I was going on tour.

ESCAPE TO NEW YORK

During the drive to California, I began to feel less sure about moving out west. My girlfriend and I were arguing a lot, and it was messing with my head in a big way. Once we got there, we lived in a Huntington Beach hotel for two weeks while I slowly started getting ready for tour. I hadn't ridden my bike in six months, but when I rode the GT ramps for practice, I regained my confidence and was once again comfortable doing tailwhips, flips, and most of my other tricks.

As the tour neared, things got worse with my girlfriend, and she flew back to Syracuse. I felt so alone. I missed my friends and family, and I hated the idea of living so far away from them. I tried to figure out the right thing to do, but finally I had to admit that California was not for me. I spelled everything out for Woody and let him know that my heart wasn't in the tour. He said he understood, so I loaded my car back up and did a marathon drive back to Syracuse in forty-five hours straight with no sleep.

MY FIVE WORST INJURIES

1. IN 1990, I broke my left shoulder learning the 540s on vert. I was in the hospital in traction for two weeks.

2. IN 1993, a drunk driver hit me. The car was going about forty-five miles an hour, and threw me fifteen feet through the air. When I landed my right shoulder was torn, my skull was fractured, and the impact had left a blood clot on my brain. I stayed in the hospital for eight days and was ordered to stay off my bike for six months.

3. IN 1995, I was doing shows at the Texas State Fair in Dallas, and it was the last show of the day. I came down from the biggest can-can I've ever done and went straight into a lookback on the other side of the ramp, which was eleven or twelve feet out. My shirt got caught on the handlebars, and I slammed from about twenty-three feet in the air. I hit so hard it tore my spleen instantly, and I got knocked out.

4. IN 1994, I went to a skatepark in Daytona Beach, Florida. I was doing a manual (coasting wheelie) from the vert wall to a brick wall just beside it. When I went to jump into the ramp, which was set out about three feet from the wall, my front end dropped, and I hooked my front wheel on the coping, which threw me straight on my head. My neck and back were screwed up from the impact.

5. IN 2001, I was practicing for the Gravity Games at Jaycee Park in Greenville, North Carolina. I did a 540-tailwhip on the vert resi and I slightly overrotated and slid sideways down the ramp. When I got to the bottom, I hit a bump in the plastic resi cover and twisted my knee, which tore my MCL.

CAN-CAN FLIP AT THE 1993 SANTA CLARA FAIR, CALIFORNIA.

TAILWHIP AIR IN MY OLD BACKYARD. I DONATED THIS RAMP TO
GREENVILLE'S JAYCEE SKATEPARK WHEN I SOLD THE HOUSE.

CHA

CHAPTER 9
MAYBE RIDING, MAYBE NOT

Once I was back home, I had no idea what I was going to do with my life. I figured that since I had no sponsor, I'd better get a job. I wound up detailing cars at a local Chevy dealer, which only lasted for two and a half days. By the middle of the third day, I'd had enough of someone telling me how to wash cars, so I went to lunch and never came back. I wasn't too concerned about money, because I had $15,000 coming from the car accident settlement, plus another $12,000 in lost wages that Woody got for me. In 1994, $27,000 was a lot of money to make in a year, so things didn't seem too bleak.

The longer I was back in New York, the less interested I became in riding. There weren't any ramps nearby, and I was starting to wonder if I should quit freestyle and move on with my life. I still enjoyed riding but couldn't really picture myself never competing again, so I decided I needed some motivation. I figured that would come when I got a good vert ramp. I was living in an apartment in Syracuse with Jim Cook, so I talked my dad into letting me build a twenty-four-foot-wide, ten-foot-tall vert ramp in his backyard. The ramp turned out exactly the way I planned it and was fun to ride, but it took forty minutes to drive to my dad's house. I also had no one to ride with, since my brother had moved to Greenville, North Carolina, earlier in the year with his girlfriend, who was going to college there. All of these things combined meant I only rode my brand-new, perfect vert ramp fifteen times.

LAZY DAYS

By September, I was barely riding my bike at all. Jim and I would occasionally ride around the city, but it was never very serious and it didn't happen very often. I was mostly partying and had put on an extra thirty pounds to prove it. I still kept in touch with my riding friends—especially Dennis McCoy, who kept telling me I was blowing it. He knew I had a future in riding, and he had a friend at Haro who would be willing to sponsor me if I sent him a videotape of my riding. I was too lazy to make a video, so I just gave Haro a call instead.

Eventually an offer came back from Haro for $500 a month, but $6,000 a year was pretty weak. I called Dennis and said, "Thanks a lot, but I'm just going to get a job at Burger King and not even bother." Dennis was persistent; he knew that if they saw a

ROCKET-BARSPIN OVER THE MORENO VALLEY HIP IN 1994. I DON'T THINK I'VE DONE THIS TRICK SINCE.

MAYBE RIDING, MAY

X-UP 180 OVER THE SPINE DURING A PHOTO SHOOT FOR *SPORTS ILLUSTRATED FOR KIDS.*

MIRRA IMAGES

video they'd up their offer. He finally made a video résumé for me out of footage from a video called *Chasing the View Off the Cliff* that included some of my best riding from that year's contests.

Thanks to the video, Haro came through with a new offer for $900 per month. I told them to raise it to a grand and they did—just like that, I was back on Haro. In hindsight, I can't believe how much Dennis had come to the rescue. When I was just starting out in freestyle he was the hero I looked up to in all the magazines, and now he was responsible for getting me sponsored and back into riding full throttle. That's something you can never say thanks for too many times.

That September I got back into the contest scene in a hurry. There were two contests left in 1994: a 2-Hip Meet the Street in Newberg, New York, and the Bicycle Stunts finals in Hoffman Estates, Illinois. Since I had barely been riding, I wasn't sure what to expect. Luckily, things went great at both contests, and I even attempted a tailwhip-flair during the street competition in the BS finals. It was official; I was back.

CHAPTE

BIG, SPRAWLED-OUT FLIP IN THE CAGE
IN WOODWARD, 1995.

R 10 GREENVILLE BOUND

CHAPTER 10
GREENVILLE-BOUND

By the end of 1994, I knew if I wanted to continue my career as a professional bike rider I had to get more focused. Living in Syracuse was fun, but I needed something to ride and someone to ride with. My brother called and asked me to come out to Greenville, North Carolina, to visit, so I drove down to check it out.

Tim and his girlfriend lived in an apartment building that was directly across the street from Greenville's Jaycee Skatepark—they could see it from their window. The park was small and there were only a few ramps, but the location was too good to be true. Tim hadn't ridden for a while, but having a skatepark that close got him right back into it. As soon as I got there, he and I went riding.

In Greenville everything felt right. Every day Tim and I would ride with his group of friends, and they were a blast to hang out with. It seemed like the perfect place to get

INVERT ON THE BEACH DURING A CALIFORNIA B3.
THE START OF A NEW BEGINNING FOR ME.

serious about riding. A few months later when the lease expired on my Syracuse apartment, I threw everything I owned in a truck and moved into an apartment directly above Tim.

From the day I arrived in Greenville, I was riding hard three or four hours a day, which was a schedule I hadn't been on since I was a kid. The city let us build even more ramps at the park, and our sessions were out of hand. My girlfriend moved to Greenville with me, but with my life being so focused on riding again, I knew things wouldn't work out between us. After a few months, we broke up and she moved back to New York. Tim and his girlfriend had broken up as well, so he and I got our own place right down the street from the park. I was doing well in contests and having a blast, so I knew I had made the right choice.

TAILWHIP TRANSFER AT THE BS FINALS IN 1994. I PULLED THIS PERFECT IN PRACTICE, BUT COULDN'T MAKE IT WORK DURING MY RUNS.

FLIP-FAKIE AT THE OLD JAYCEE SKATEPARK IN 1996. I DON'T FLIP FAKIE MUCH ANYMORE. IT'S A DIFFERENT SPIN THAN THE FLAIR, SO I LEFT IT ALONE.

CAN-CAN LOOKBACK DURING A SHOW AT MAGIC MOUNTAIN IN CALIFORNIA IN 1995. I GOT TO RIDE THE ROLLER COASTERS BETWEEN DEMOS.

FLAT 360 OVER THE MOST JACKED-UP SPINE OF ALL TIME IN HAMPTON, VIRGINIA, IN 1995. I DON'T KNOW HOW I GOT THIS HIGH OR THIS FLAT OVER THAT CRAPPY RAMP.

JUST UNDER THIRTEEN FEET OUT OF THE RAMP DURING A
K2 HIGH-AIR CONTEST AT WOODWARD.

THE RISE OF THE X

MIRRA IMAGES

14
14
14

13
13

12

14

1
11

PTER 11

2
PRO

ARD. WOODWARD. WOODWARD.

I n early 1995, word got out among riders that ESPN was planning a huge pro-only invitational contest that summer in Newport, Rhode Island. The event was billed as an "extreme sports Olympics," and it included everything—BMX, skateboarding, inline skating, bungee jumping, rock climbing—anything ESPN decided was extreme. Television networks and freestyle contests seemed like a strange mix, and everyone in BMX had serious doubts. We all thought

ESPN was doing the event to make a quick buck, and we figured it would never last. I was invited to ride in the vert contest, so I was willing to give it a try.

From the minute I got to the Extreme Games it had a completely different feel than any other contest I'd been to. I was used to contests in existing skateparks where everyone in the building was a rider. Now I was riding in a historic fort for a TV show complete with a live audience and TV cameras everywhere.

Despite the skepticism, the Extreme Games turned out to be an amazing event, and it gave freestyle more mainstream exposure than ever before. I got second place in vert behind Mat Hoffman, and that came with a check for $1,000—the most money I'd ever won in a single contest. (Second place in a BS event would have netted $200.) For all of us who were trying to make a living riding our bikes, it seemed like a glimmer of hope at the end of a long, dark tunnel.

At the end of 1995, Mat Hoffman announced that the freestyle contest scene was going to change the following year because ESPN was getting involved in a big way. The network had teamed up with contest promoters in BMX, skateboarding, and inline skating to form Destination Extreme, a five-contest series that would be held in locations around the United States and would determine who got to compete in the Extreme Games. ESPN planned to hold the Games in the fall of 1996, but changed the name to the X Games. Every event ESPN had planned was going to be televised, which meant freestyle would get even more exposure.

Timingwise, things couldn't have happened any better for me. I had only started riding hard again three months earlier. Who knows where I would be now if my comeback had been a little off.

A NEW STYLE IS BORN

Since all of the contests were now going to air on TV, I decided it was time to change the way I rode. My normal contest runs were working well and I was winning a lot, but I wanted to show the world that freestylers were true athletes and not just kids on bikes who were throwing themselves in the air. During what had become a normal contest run, riders would do a hard trick or two, stop and rest, and then start going again. I wanted my runs to look incredible from the second I started riding until the second I was done, so I came up with a plan. My runs would flow nonstop with hard tricks being fired out the entire way. I wanted to mix in lip tricks—grinds and tricks done on the deck of the ramp—in an all-new way,

NOTHING OVER THE BOX IN FAIRMONT PARK, PENNSYLVANIA, IN 1996 DURING MY YELLOW BIKE PHASE.

Mirra image

especially on vert. Typically riders did lip tricks when they screwed up during a run and lost their momentum, but I wanted to do high-speed lip tricks straight into big airs so the run was full of variety. I also put a lot of time into doing airs on vert, turning opposite the direction I usually did. Turning both ways on a ramp sounds simple, but every rider inherently turns in one direction or the other, and going the opposite way is like throwing a baseball with your wrong hand. A few riders were doing occasional opposite airs, but I wanted to be able to do it comfortably while still doing big tricks. Contest runs lasted between seventy-five and ninety seconds, and to ride wide open for that long takes everything you've got. I decided to get myself in shape, so I hit the gym and put my plan into motion.

Once I started riding with my new style, the wins poured in, starting with the first Destination Extreme event in South Padre Island, Texas. The judges loved the nonstop barrage of hard tricks on street, and it wasn't long before other riders were riding the same way.

OLYMPIC GLORY

ESPN gave freestyle so much airtime that the public had taken notice and high-profile demos were popping up all over the place. I had ridden in tons of big shows over the years, and in the summer of 1996 I was invited to perform in a demo during the closing ceremony of the summer Olympics along with Mat Hoffman, Dennis McCoy, Taj Mihelich, Steve Swope, Rick Thorne, and Joe Rich. We all went to Atlanta, Georgia, a week early to prepare for the show and came up with a highly choreographed routine on a myriad of connected ramps.

When it was time for the show to start and we walked our bikes into the Olympic stadium, the feeling was unreal. The capacity crowd was so loud that it sounded more like roars than cheers. Thousands of camera flashes

image

UNDERGROUND
SKATEBOARD PARK

TABLETOP AT THE NEW MEXICO STATE FAIR IN 1995. THAT'S KENAN HARKIN IN THE BACKGROUND, ANNOUNCING.

were going off, and the adrenaline was pumping like crazy. I was more nervous at that moment than at any contest I'd ever ridden in, but we all managed to hold it together and put on an amazing show.

When we finished, we were all on the verge of tears. It may sound weird, but riding in the closing ceremonies at the Olympics in front of that many people is a big deal whether you want to admit it or not. Our show may have lasted only six minutes, but we will remember it for the rest of our lives.

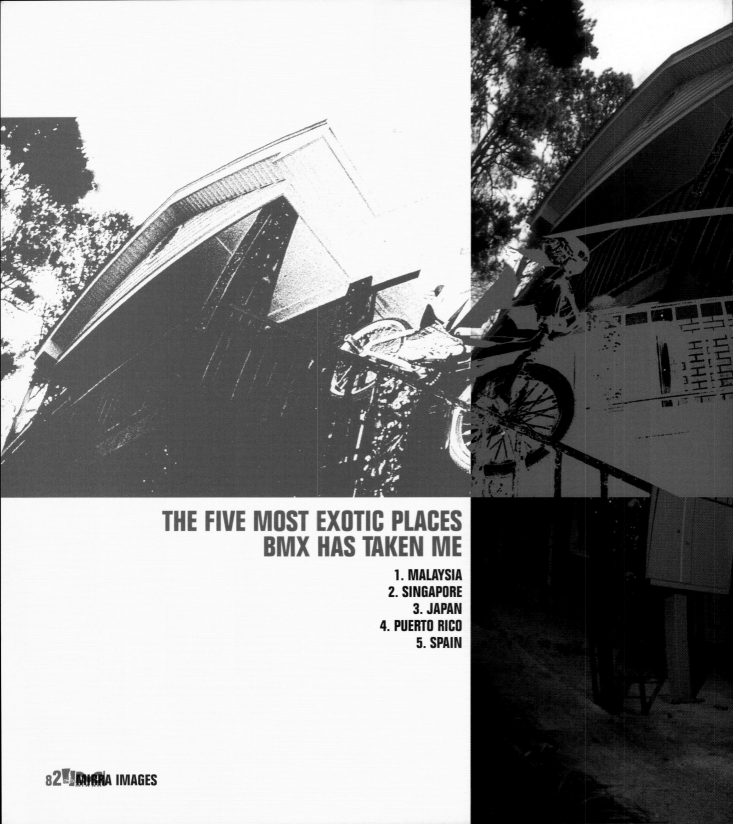

THE FIVE MOST EXOTIC PLACES
BMX HAS TAKEN ME

1. MALAYSIA
2. SINGAPORE
3. JAPAN
4. PUERTO RICO
5. SPAIN

RAIL SLIDE IN GREENVILLE. AKA MAKING FRIENDS WITH APARTMENT DWELLERS.

CHA

FUFANU IN THE CAGE, WOODWARD STYLE.

SKATEPARKS AND SLIM JIM
CHAPTER 12

ESPN's contests were rolling strong in 1997, and bike riding's popularity was growing fast. More money started coming in from sponsors, and the better the riders placed at TV contests, the more they were worth. I had a pretty competitive drive and was getting a lot of TV time, so the scenario was working well for me. Before TV got involved, I treated contests as an excuse to party with my friends, but now I was staying mellow to focus on what I wanted to do. It made contests a tad more boring than what I was used to, but the wins were proving it was worth it.

QUARTERPIPE TAILWHIP DURING A TYPICAL SESSION AT JAYCEE SKATEPARK.

SKATEPARKS AND SLIM JIM

WALLRIDE AT BACKDOOR IN GREENVILLE—
THE SMALLEST SKATEPARK I'VE EVER RIDDEN.

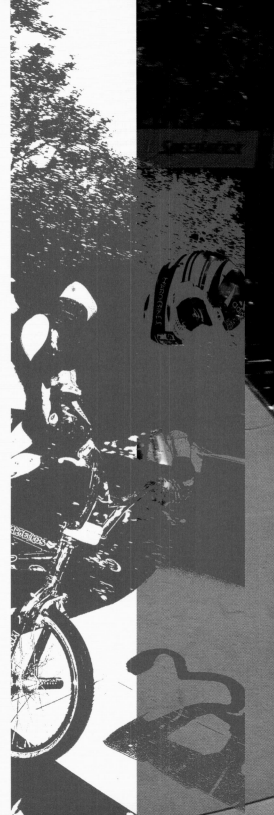

Another thing on my mind that year was opening a skatepark in Raleigh, North Carolina. My friends Don Wigent and Kerry McElwee were looking for suitable buildings, but the costs were through the roof. Kerry had spoken to Slim Jim about helping fund the park, since they were based in Raleigh. I gave Slim Jim's marketing department a call about the park too and told them I was looking for personal sponsorships as well.

Costs in Raleigh turned out to be so high that the skatepark plan eventually fell through, but Slim Jim's marketing department was still interested in me. We worked out a deal where they gave me $2,500 for sponsorship for the 1997 X Games, and in return I put a big Slim Jim sticker on the front of my helmet. Our deal was for that contest only, but I left the sticker on after the X Games ended and started talking to Slim Jim about doing something more long term. The marketing people were into it, and to this day Slim Jim is still one of the best sponsors I've ever had.

EASTWOOD SKATEPARK

In early 1998, Don and I found out about a 12,000-square-foot building in Wilmington, North Carolina—two hours from Greenville—that could work as a park. The lease on the building was $5,000 per month and building ramps would be expensive, but we knew we could make it work. To get the park off the ground we came up with $14,000 each, and Slim Jim signed on as a partner and kicked in another fourteen grand.

The doors officially opened at Eastwood on April 4—my birthday. Even though the park was open to the public during the day, since we owned it, we could ride it after hours

VERT NOSE-WHEELIE IN 1997, BACK WHEN
FRONT BRAKES WERE A LOT OF FUN.

when the park was closed. There were a few offices in the building, so Don and I each claimed one, got a shower built, and called it home to avoid paying rent for an apartment. Luckily, the fire marshal never knew a thing.

Once Eastwood was up and running, it didn't take long for us to learn that making money in the skatepark business is not easy. A lot of kids were paying to ride the park, but we were only bringing in enough revenue to pay the bills and not enough to pay either of us a salary. To make things even more complicated, I was on the road nonstop for contests and demos, which meant Don was basically married to the park without making any money.

After eight months, Don and I were over the skatepark business. Having our own warehouse full of ramps was great for riding, but as a business it was impossible. I finally decided to give my share of the park to a friend who had been helping us out, and Don sold his shares as well. The park managed to stay open for two more years, but eventually it closed down altogether.

HARO AD FROM THE FIRST DESTINATION EXTREME IN SOUTH PADRE ISLAND, TEXAS.

miracle whip

'96 Freestyle World Champion-Vert
'96 X-Games Champion-Street
'96 X-Games 2nd-Vert

'96 B.S. Series Champion-Street
'96 B.S. Series 2nd-Vert

dave mirra

EXPERIMENTING WITH A FRAMESTAND ICEPICK ON WOODWARD'S SUB RAIL IN 1997.

FLAIR AT SCRAP IN HOFFMAN ESTATES, ILLINOIS, IN 1997. FOUR YEARS EARLIER, I PULLED MY FIRST FLAIR ON THIS SAME RAMP.

IN 1997 I REINTRODUCED THE WALLTAP TO BMX.

EASTWOOD SKATEPARK

In early 1998, Don and I found out about a 13,000-square-foot building in Wilmington, North Carolina—two hours from Greenville—that could work as a park. The lease on the building was $5,000 per month and building ramps would be expensive, but we knew we could make it work. To pull the park off the ground we came up with $14,000 each, and Don signed on as a partner and kicked in another fourteen grand.

The doors officially opened at Eastwood on April 4—my birthday. Even though the park was open to the public during the day, since we owned it, we could ride it after hours when the park was closed. There were a few offices in the building, so Don and I each claimed one, got a shower built, and called it home to avoid paying rent for an apartment. Luckily, the fire marshal never knew a thing.

Once Eastwood was up and running, it didn't take long for us to learn that making money in the skatepark business is not easy. A lot of kids were paying to ride the park, but we were only bringing in enough revenue to pay the bills, not enough to pay either of us a salary. To make things even more complicated, I was on the road nonstop for contests and demos, which meant Don was basically married to the park without making any money.

After eight months, Don and I were over the skatepark business. Having our own warehouse full of ramps was great for my riding, but as a business it was impossible. I finally decided to give my share of the park to a friend who had been helping me out, and Don sold his shares as well. The park managed to stay open for two more years, but eventually it closed down altogether.

ESPN's contests were rolling around in 1997, and this riding's popularity was growing fast. More money started coming in from sponsors, and the bigger the riders placed at TV contests, the more they were worth. I had a pretty sweet setup going from all of my TV time, so the scenario was working well for me. Before TV got involved, I treated contests as a house party with my friends, but now I was staying mellow to focus on what I wanted to do. It made contests a lot more boring than what I used to, but the wins were proving it was worth it.

Another thing in my deal that year was Grappling a skatepark in Raleigh, North Carolina. My friends Don Wigwet and Kerry McElwee were looking for suitable buildings, but the costs were through the roof. Kerry had spoken to Slim Jim about helping fund the park, since they were located in Raleigh. I gave Slim Jim's marketing department a call about the park too and told them I was looking for personal sponsorships as well.

Costs in Raleigh turned out to be so high that the skatepark plan eventually fell through, but Slim Jim's marketing department was still interested in me. We worked out a deal, where they gave me $2,500 to sponsor me for the 1997 X Games, and in return I put a big Slim Jim sticker on the front of my helmet. Our deal was for that contest only, but I left the sticker on after the X Games ended and started talking to Slim Jim about doing something more long-term. The marketing people were into it, and to this day Slim Jim is still one of the best sponsors I've ever had.

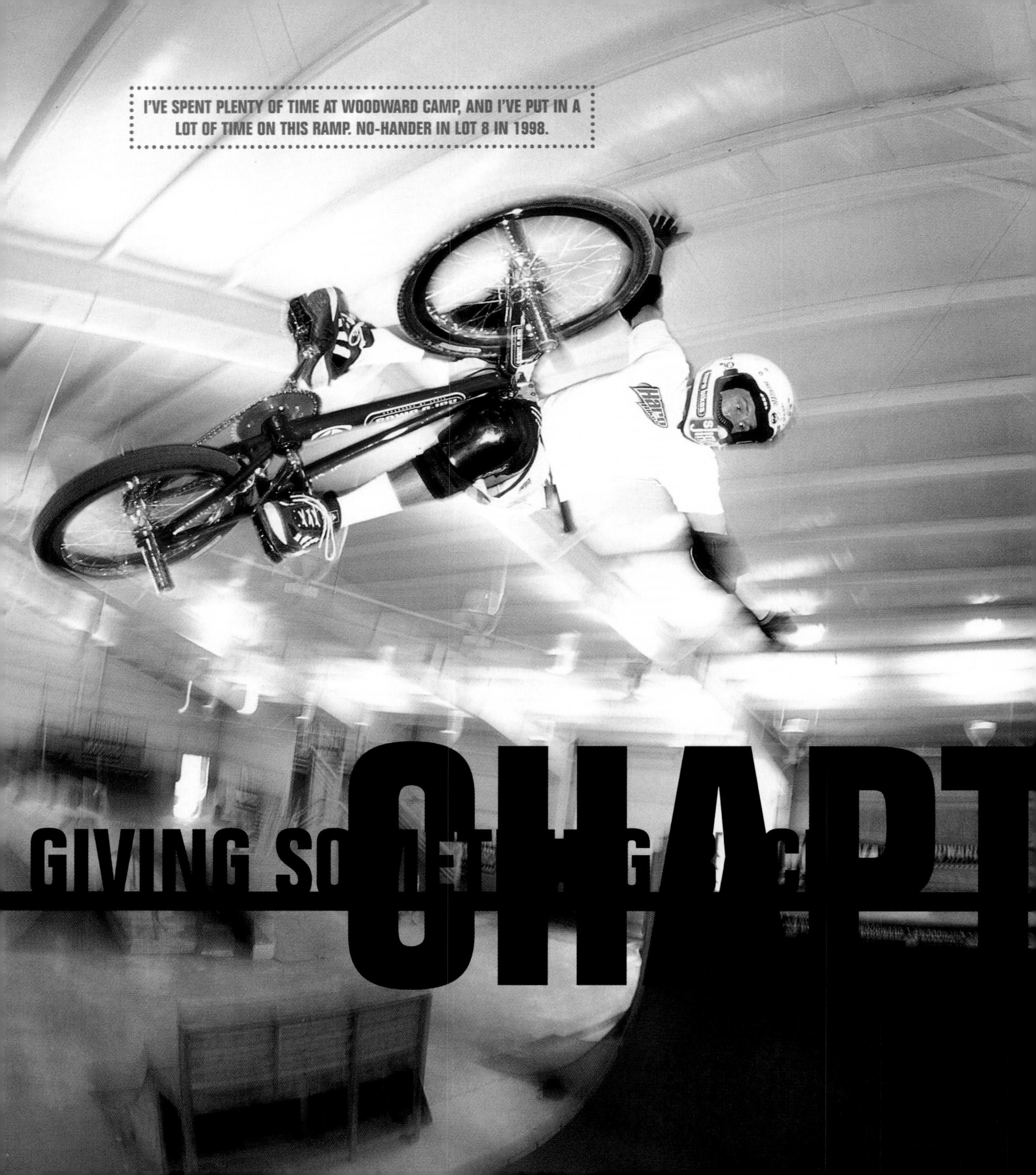

I'VE SPENT PLENTY OF TIME AT WOODWARD CAMP, AND I'VE PUT IN A LOT OF TIME ON THIS RAMP. NO-HANDER IN LOT 8 IN 1998.

CHAPT

GIVING SOMETHING BACK

While visiting family in Syracuse in early 1998, I picked up a realty circular and took it back to Wilmington with me. I was flipping through it one day when I came across a three-bedroom, two-story house for $70,000 that was perfect for my mom, who had been renting places ever since she and my dad divorced. I was making good money and had saved a lot of it, so I knew I could afford to buy the place. I gave the real estate agent a call, made an appointment, and then drove thirteen hours to Syracuse to check it out. When I saw the house in person, I knew I had to get it. I went through all the paperwork, and then tried to control myself so I wouldn't ruin the surprise.

The next day I was so excited that I could barely keep myself under control. I went to visit my mom and casually said, "Mom, let's go for a drive." She had no idea where we were going, and I made sure our route took us straight to the new house. When we pulled up, I pointed at the house and said, "See that house? You can move in in a month." She couldn't believe it, and all I could do was smile. It was one of the most important moments in my life. My mom had given me so much—a lifetime of love and support. To be able to give something back to her was like a dream, and the fact that it all came from bike riding made it that much sweeter.

CHAPTER 13
GIVING SOMETHING BACK

ER 13

DOING LIFESTYLE PHOTO SHOOTS ALWAYS
FEELS WEIRD, BUT IT'S PART OF THE JOB.

TAKING A BREAK FROM THE RAMPS TO RIDE
DIRT AT THE 401 TRAILS IN RALEIGH.

THE FIRST DOUBLE FLIP EVER PULLED IN A
CONTEST AND ON A REAL RAMP.
UTOPIA SKATEPARK IN RALEIGH,
NORTH CAROLINA, IN 2000.

A DREAM COME TRUE: MY FIRST HOUSE, IN 1999.

TABLE-360 OVER THE JAYCEE SKATEPARK SPINE. DOING THIS TRICK HIGH AND NOSING THE BIKE BACK IN IS ONE OF THE BEST FEELINGS OF ALL TIME.

NO-HANDED SPINE 360. THIS PHOTO WOUND UP IN MY SECOND *RIDE* INTERVIEW.

HOME SWEET HOME

A few months later I was back in my apartment in Greenville. A pro named Mike Laird had moved to town, and a few other pros were moving there as well. We were all friends and had a great scene going, so I started thinking about buying a house for myself. After a lot of thought, I came to the conclusion that I really liked brick houses and wanted at least an acre of land so that I could build a vert ramp in the backyard. The search was on.

Not long after I started looking, I saw a house advertised in the paper that seemed to be what I was looking for. Then while walking by a real estate office, I spotted a brochure for the exact same house sitting on a desk. That kind of coincidence seemed like a sign, so I talked to the broker and worked out a deal. Within a few months, the house was mine, and I built my own private vert ramp in the backyard.

After riding my new ramp for a few months, I had an idea for a vert training ramp that would help me improve even more. I wanted to create a ramp on which I could take off from a regular vert ramp but land on a ramp that was not nearly as steep. With a setup like that I could go for hard tricks, but since my landing wouldn't be as steep, I wouldn't have to land perfectly. I told Gary Ream, one of the owners of Woodward Camp, about the idea and his eyes immediately lit up.

At Woodward, to help kids learn jumping tricks, they built a jump ramp consisting of a normal takeoff and a pit filled with foam cubes for the landing. The foam pit was used to let riders get comfortable trying tricks in the air, and once they were confident jumping into the foam they could move on to the resi box jump. The resi had a normal takeoff, and the landing was a soft foam pad covered by a piece of resi material that allowed riders to ride away if they pulled a trick. If they crashed, the foam underneath the resi absorbed most of the impact so riders wouldn't get hurt. By using the foam pit and the resi, riders were able to learn tricks that would have beaten them up if they started out on a regular box jump.

When Gary heard my idea about the vert ramp, he suggested that the landing be covered with a foam pad and resi like they used on the camp's resi box jump. He said that he would even build a ramp like that at

FRONT BRAKES IN EFFECT. FRAMESTAND-TWEAKER-NOSEPICK IN 1998.

Woodward, and if it worked out he would give me a free vert resi section for my backyard ramp in Greenville. That sounded good to me, so Woodward built a resi section at the end of an indoor vert ramp and it worked well. Gary was stoked, and he came through with a free resi for the ramp in my backyard.

TEAMMATE/ROOMMATE

Haro added another pro rider, Ryan Nyquist, to its team in 1998, and he and I became good friends. Ryan lived in Los Gatos, California, and was looking for a change of scenery, so I invited him to check out the Greenville scene and move in with me for a few months. He liked the idea, and in a month he was living in one of my spare bedrooms.

Having Ryan live with me was a lot of fun, but at the same time we had our problems. We were traveling together nonstop, and when we came home from an event we were *still* together. We were competing against each other all the time, so living under the same roof was getting tense. Ryan was stoked on Greenville, and since he was making good money, I told him he should look into buying a house for himself. Coincidentally, there was one only a few blocks away that was on the market, so I called the realty broker and set things in motion. A month later, Ryan was a neighbor instead of a roommate.

AN ALL-NEW FAMILIE

Toward the end of 1998, the money I was making was getting incredible, but with all of the contest wins and the coverage I was getting, I had no idea how much I was really worth. I had a manager who was supposed to get endorsements for me and handle my contracts, but a new agent, Steve Astephen, was approaching me to work with him. Steve wasn't messing around, and the deals his firm, called The Familie, brought to the table were too good to be true. As my agent, Steve would take a portion of what I earned, but he was raising my salary ceiling so high that he was worth every penny. After working with Steve on a few deals, I told my old manager I was leaving and signed with The Familie. It turned out to be one of the best moves I've ever made. Steve has become one of the best friends I've ever had, and you can't ask for a better business relationship than that.

DAVE MIRRA'S FREESTYLE BMX

In 1999, before I was even officially working with The Familie, Steve approached me about a project he was working on with Akklaim for a Dave Mirra video game. I've always been a video game junkie, so the opportunity to have my own was way too good to pass up.

FLIPS ARE ONE OF THE HARDEST TRICKS YOU CAN DO OVER A
DOUBLE-COPING SPINE AND STILL LAND SMOOTH. THIS IS A
X-UP VERSION AT THE JAYCEE SKATEPARK IN 2000.

ESPN HELD ITS FIRST AND LAST VERT DOUBLES CONTEST FOR BIKES AT THE 1998 X GAMES. I RODE WITH DENNIS MCCOY AND WE TOOK THE WIN WITH AIRS LIKE THIS. DENNIS ALSO STOOD ON THE DECK OF THE RAMP WHILE I TAILTAPPED HIS BACK.

SIGNATURE SERIES FRAME

<TESTING>

<MOTIVATION>

<RYAN AT WORK>

<TESTING>

<HOME>

<TRASH DAY>

THIS MAY BE THE ONLY BMX AD TO FEATURE
A GUY JUMPING OVER A LAWNMOWER.

MADE IN USA
NYQUIST CRMO PRO FRAME
AVAILABLE IN SKY BLUE AND
CANDY GREEN

backtrail
haro bikes

backtrail
haro bikes

MADE IN USA
MIRRA CRMO PRO FRAME
AVAILABLE IN CANDY RED
AND PEARL WHITE

adidas
BMX
mervyn's California
BOBS

Official Team Co-Sponsors

FOR ME, FLIPS WERE BECOMING A NORMAL TRICK OVER SPINE BY THE 2000 X GAMES.

Getting to see how the *Dave Mirra's Freestyle BMX* game was made before it hit the shelves was a pretty cool experience. They asked me for a list of riders I'd like to feature in the game with me, so I picked people I really liked and respected and asked if they were interested. No one turned the offer down. Ryan Nyquist was one of the riders featured in the game, and we both went to Woodward Camp to do motion capture work. We put on Spandex suits covered with special Ping-Pong balls, and then we did all of our tricks while infrared cameras that only saw the balls translated our moves and fed them into a computer. We had to do every trick we knew on both a box jump and vert ramp, and that turned out to be the hardest part of the entire process. We also went to a studio in California so they could scan our heads to make our animated characters in the game look as real as possible. A camera rotated 360 degrees around our heads, and if we blinked or moved in the slightest it would mess up the image and we'd have to start over.

BRAKELESS NOSEPICKS ON VERT SHOULDN'T BE POSSIBLE, BUT THEY ARE IF YOU HAVE A LOT OF CONFIDENCE, BALANCE, AND LUCK.

MY FIRST PRIVATE TRAINING FACILITY—PLAYING VIDEO GAMES IN MY OLD LIVING ROOM.

MBNA IMAGES

360-TAILWHIP OVER RYAN NYQUIST'S SPINE. A SHOT
JUST LIKE THIS RAN ON THE COVER OF *RIDE* MAGAZINE.

TAKING A BREAK AT A CONTEST TO GET
MY THOUGHTS TOGETHER.

Dave's

Collect them all!
Series 1:

Haro Dave Mirra Signature Series

GT Tour

Haro Ryan Nyquist Backflip Pro

GT Speed Series

ROAD CHAMPS BXS

Hade's Bike

Collect them all! Series 1:

The ORIGINAL Trick Stick Bike

The Best Bikes...
The Best Riders:
Mirra
Nyquist
Foster
Garcia

The Trick Stick makes it Sick.
Trick Stick works as wrench, bikestand and trick performer.

HAVING A SIGNATURE BMX BIKE IS COOL, BUT GETTING MY OWN SIGNITURE FINGER BIKE AND ACTION FIGURE WAS OUT OF HAND.

The Trick Stick makes it Sick.
Trick Stick works as wrench, bikestand and trick performer.

ROAD CHAMPS

TO BE ABLE TO BUILD A CUSTOM HOUSE AND PAY FOR IT BY RIDING A BIKE IS PRETTY UNREAL. I DON'T THINK MY SIXTH-GRADE TEACHER EVER SAW THIS COMING.

MY POOL HOUSE DOUBLES AS BOTH A GYM AND A PLACE FOR FRIENDS TO STAY.

I'M REALLY SERIOUS ABOUT TRAINING, SO I BUILT A PERSONAL WEIGHT ROOM IN MY POOL HOUSE. WHEN I'M IN TOWN, I TRY TO WORK OUT FOUR OR FIVE TIMES A WEEK.

I'VE ALWAYS BEEN A BIG CAR FAN. MY CURRENT LINEUP LOOKS LIKE THIS: A 2003 RANGE ROVER, 2002 BMW 745I WITH BLACK 22S, AND A SALEEN S351 SPEEDSTER MUSTANG.

MY SALEEN S351 SPEEDSTER MUSTANG. STEVE SALEEN PERSONALLY PRESENTED THIS CAR TO ME IN 2000.

MTV CRIBS CAME TO MY NEW HOUSE IN FEBRUARY TO SEE WHAT I HAD GOING ON.

HAVING A RAMP IN MY BACKYARD MADE FOR SOME CONVENIENT
SESSIONS. CAN-CAN LOOKBACK OUT BACK IN 1999.

When the game was released, the response was great. The first version sold more than one million copies, and in 2001 we released a second version with better graphics, better levels, and more riders. Everyone involved in the project got paid pretty well, and for the rest of their lives they get to tell people that they are a character in a video game. That's pretty cool by itself.

MOVIN' ON UP . . .

By 2000, my bank account was seeing numbers I never thought were possible. I was happy with the house I was living in, but with things going so well I was ready for a bigger investment. I had found an incredible neighborhood with some amazing custom-built homes in Greenville, and I knew it was the place for me. I bought an open lot in the community, found a builder to work with, and then started construction in November.

Everything about the house was custom designed, from the open floor plan and putting the master bedroom on the ground level (for easy access in case I get hurt) to a pool house that has a gym on the first floor and a loft

for guests on the second. This was home. I sold my old house and donated my backyard vert ramp to Jaycee Skatepark. This way I still had a vert ramp to ride, but I didn't feel as if riding followed me home at the end of the day. Having ramps in my backyard was a dream at first, but I learned that just having regular access to good ramps was all I really needed.

MY OWN PRIVATE HEAVEN

That year, the level of riding in the pro class was unreal, and I started thinking about ways to progress even further. I still rode Greenville's Jaycee Skatepark and a few other private ramps around town for variety, but I had some bigger ideas.

Having access to resi and foam raises a person's level of vert riding in a hurry, but a rider would have to have regular access to them or he wouldn't be able to keep up with everyone else. Mat Hoffman had a vert resi and a vert foam pit setup at his warehouse in Oklahoma City, and

FLIPPING THE SPINE WHILE FILMING A
COMMERCIAL FOR MY FIRST VIDEO GAME.

NEAR-DEATH FUFANU, SALT LAKE CITY
VANS TRIPLE CROWN.

THIS IS ONE OF MY FAVORITE INDIAN AIRS OF
ALL TIME—I JUST LIKE THE STYLE.

Woodward had its own facility that a lot of pros had access to. Since donating my vert ramp and resi to Greenville's Jaycee Skatepark, the resi portion had been destroyed by the weather. What I needed was a private, indoor, local spot to build my own ramp setup, but I had a lot more on my mind than vert.

There aren't many warehouses in Greenville with high enough roofs to build a vert ramp inside, so I bought a piece of land and had a custom warehouse built from scratch. I paid for the land and the building, but luckily I had help paying for the ramps. My sponsors, Fox Racing, DC Shoes, and Bell Helmets, helped out a lot, and then Gary Ream had his Woodward construction crew come down to build the resi and foam pits. I wanted the surface of every ramp to be layered with a ramp-specific material called Skatelite, which is durable and fast but costs $200 per sheet. I talked to Jack Murphy, a great friend and a well-known ramp builder, who said he had a solution. If I paid for a truck to haul it, I could have all the Skatelite used on the 2002 Gravity Games ramps in Cleveland, Ohio—for free. That was more than 200 sheets of free Skatelite. I said thanks and got a truck immediately.

Building the ramps in the warehouse took six months, and it could not have turned out better. When construction was finished I had a vert ramp with foam and resi sections, box jumps with foam and resi, and a wallride foam pit and resi that I designed, plus a resi spine ramp.

From the day the ramps were built, new tricks were getting fired out. The wallride foam and resi allowed me to try any wallride trick that came to mind, and I was finding ways to make them work. The ramps in the warehouse are still relatively new, so I can't even imagine how far the warehouse is going to push my riding.

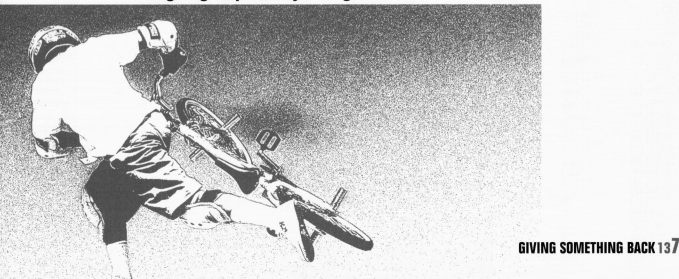

TWO OF MY FAVORITE THINGS IN ONE AD: RIDING AND GOLF.

adidas

adidas

- GOLD MEDAL VERT
- GOLD MEDAL STREET
- GOLD MEDAL VERT DOUBLES
- MALE ATHLETE OF THE GAMES

1998 BICYCLE STUNT SERIES
- OVERALL CHAMPION VERT
- OVERALL CHAMPION STREET

1997 ESPN X GAMES
- GOLD MEDAL VERT
- GOLD MEDAL STREET

1997 BICYCLE STUNT SERIES
- OVERALL CHAMPION VERT
- OVERALL CHAMPION STREET

1996 ESPN X GAMES
- GOLD MEDAL STREET
- SILVER MEDAL VERT

1995 ESPN X GAMES
- SILVER MEDAL VERT

DAVE MIRRA

Photos: Pete Demos

Haro Bikes   1230 Avenida Chelsea   Vista, CA 92083   760-599-0544   www.harobikes.com

Haro Bikes

AT A SOUL BOWL CONTEST IN 2000 A TV CAMERAMAN PUT A BOOM CAMERA TOO FAR OVER THE LIP OF THE RAMP DURING MY FIRST RUN. I HIT IT ON ONE OF MY FIRST AIRS AND WOUND UP DROPPING FIFTEEN FEET TO THE BOTTOM OF THE THE BOWL. LUCKILY THERE WERE NO CAMERAS IN THE WAY DURING THIS INVERT.

MIRRA IMAGES

EVENING-SESSION TAILTAP ON
WOODWARD'S VERT WALL IN 1998.

MY MOST RECENT PROJECT WAS A PERSONAL RIDING FACILITY THAT CONSISTED OF FOAM PITS, RESI RAMPS, AND EVERYTHING THAT WOULD HELP ME RIDE AT A HIGHER LEVEL. FROM THE DAY THE RAMPS WENT UP, THIS HAS BEEN MY SECOND HOME.

MIRRA IMAGES

BARSPIN-TO-SUICIDE NO-HANDER IN ANAHEIM.
YOU LET GO OF THE BARS WHEN YOU'RE COMING IN, SO
IT'S A PRETTY SCARY TRICK.

No other bike is equipped with

GOLD MEDALS ALWAYS KEEP
YOUR SPONSORS HAPPY.

haro bikes

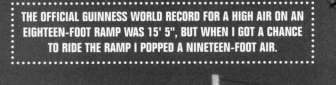

THE OFFICIAL GUINNESS WORLD RECORD FOR A HIGH AIR ON AN
EIGHTEEN-FOOT RAMP WAS 15' 5", BUT WHEN I GOT A CHANCE
TO RIDE THE RAMP I POPPED A NINETEEN-FOOT AIR.

CHAPTER

14

Action sports athletes were getting pretty well known by 2001, but there was one string attached: you had to do well at the big televised contests if you wanted to be seen on TV. The problem was that the contest coverage was only showing what we could do on our bikes, but they never showed who we were as individuals. The public was getting a lopsided view of riding, and a lot of amazing riders who didn't enter contests were getting overlooked. I wanted to do something to change that.

I came up with a tour and series of TV shows that would feature incredible riding and show what we were like off our bikes. ESPN covered a similar skateboard tour called Tony Hawk's Giant Skatepark Tour the year before, and that was the model for what I wanted to accomplish. I had done hundreds of demos in the past, but they were usually punk rock–style tours with a van and the cheapest hotels we could find. This time we had a luxury tour bus, nice hotels, and an ESPN camera crew documenting everything. It was dubbed The Dave Mirra BMX Super Tour, and we left in the spring for the first of a three-leg tour.

The riding that went down was intense, but since most of the riders were my friends from Greenville, they had similar styles and didn't come off as very diverse. A lot of them took it as a chance to prove themselves on TV, so everything on tour revolved around riding. The guys would ride all night

TYPICAL AUTOGRAPH SESSION DURING THE SUPER TOUR. SOMETIMES THE AUTOGRAPH SESSIONS LASTED LONGER THAN THE DEMOS.

SPROCKET SLIDE ON THE EAST CAROLINA UNIVERSITY
CAMPUS. I WAS FEELING STREET THAT DAY.

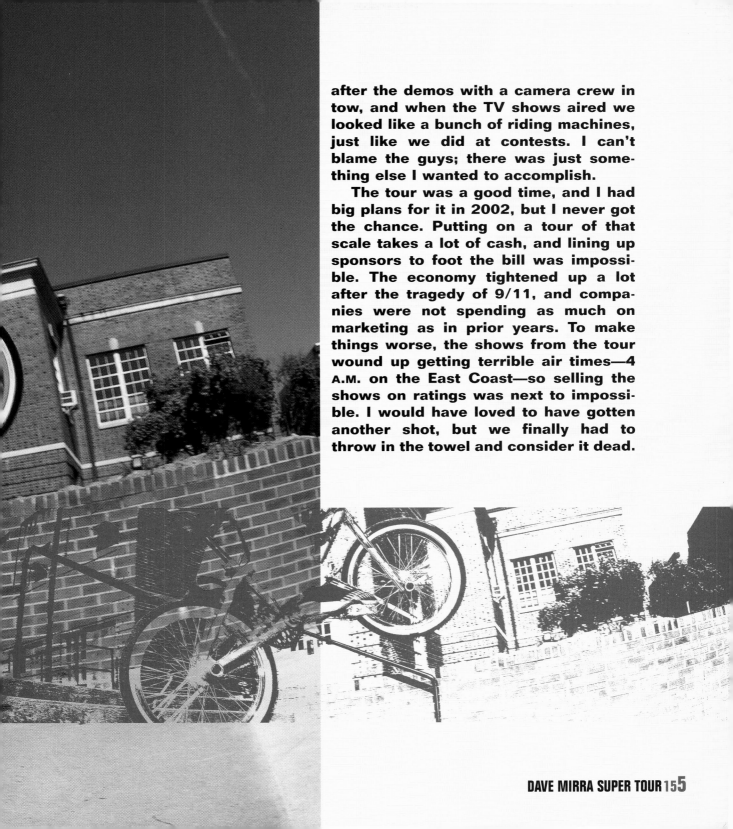

after the demos with a camera crew in tow, and when the TV shows aired we looked like a bunch of riding machines, just like we did at contests. I can't blame the guys; there was just something else I wanted to accomplish.

The tour was a good time, and I had big plans for it in 2002, but I never got the chance. Putting on a tour of that scale takes a lot of cash, and lining up sponsors to foot the bill was impossible. The economy tightened up a lot after the tragedy of 9/11, and companies were not spending as much on marketing as in prior years. To make things worse, the shows from the tour wound up getting terrible air times—4 A.M. on the East Coast—so selling the shows on ratings was next to impossible. I would have loved to have gotten another shot, but we finally had to throw in the towel and consider it dead.

TAKING A MINI RAMP TRICK TO VERT IN ESCONDIDO FOR A DC PHOTO SHOOT IN 2001.

ON THE ROAD FOR THE 2001 DAVE
MIRRA BMX SUPER TOUR.

BARSPIN-TO-ONE-HAND TWEAKER IN
2001 IN ESCONDIDO, CALIFORNIA.

MUSIC TO TOUR BY: MY FAVORITE BANDS

1. **SOCIAL DISTORTION**
2. **MÖTLEY CRÜE**
3. **BRUCE SPRINGSTEEN**
4. **JOURNEY**
5. **THE BEATLES**

CONTEMPLATING SUICIDE WITH DANNY WAY AT THE DC SUPER RAMP IN SAN DIEGO.

THE DC SUPER RAMP WAS GOOD FOR MORE THAN JUST BIG AIRS. BUNNYHOP-BARSPIN DROP-IN.

POST CONTEST AUTOGRAPH SESSION IN ATLANTA.

THE SUPER TOUR WASN'T ONLY ABOUT RIDING. HERE ROB WELLS, RYAN NYQUIST, ME, AND DAVE OSATO TAKE A GOLF BREAK IN ATLANTA.

TAILWHIP OVER THE CHANNEL IN 2001 AT THE
HOME OF THE CALIFORNIA ANGELS

TAKING A BREAK WHILE STREET RIDING IN NEW YORK. THIS PHOTO ALSO GOT USED ON THE COVER OF THE DAVE MIRRA'S TRICK TIPS VIDEO.

I OFFICIALLY WENT PLATINUM. GOLD MEDAL PHOTO SHOOT FOR MY FIRST DC AD.

HEAVY METALS ADE

CHA

CHAPTER 15
HEAVY MEDALS AND THINGS TO COME

I've had a good run at contests like the X Games, and it turns out that I've won more X Games gold medals than any X Games athlete in any other sport. The media likes to play that up and I am proud of it, but that was never my goal. I have a competitive nature, but I just take it contest by contest and try to ride the best I can. There are times when I think I've accomplished enough and wonder why I stress about contests so much. By now I should be going to contests to ride and have fun, but that competitive drive is always there. It's like there's a voice in the back of my head saying, "How can you be satisfied with fourth place when you have the ability to win?" My hardest competition is always with myself.

The medals and the contest wins are all awesome, but those really aren't the reasons I'm riding. The truth is that riding my bike has always been the best creative release I know. On my bike I have the freedom to do anything I put my mind to, and that's what I live for. If I go too long without riding I start to get tense, but learning a new trick snaps me right back into shape.

AIRS OUT OF A VERT WALL ARE A LOT HARDER THAN OUT OF A TYPICAL VERT RAMP. X-UP AT THE 2000 X GAMES IN SAN FRANCISCO.

STRAIGHT TAILWHIP DOWN THE SKI JUMP AT THE 2002 X GAMES.

WALLRIDE-TO-WHIP OFF AN EIGHT-FOOT
QUARTER AT THE 2002 X GAMES.

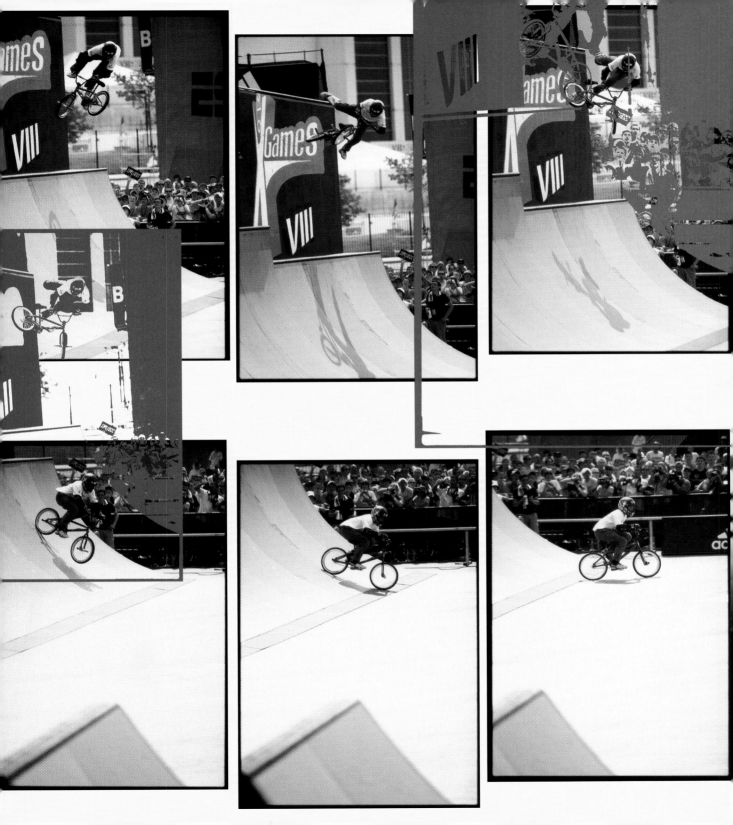

THE HUCK JAM

In 2002, I got a call about going on a new tour called the Tony Hawk Boom Boom Huck Jam. It was going to be a full-blown stadium tour that featured BMX bike riders and skateboarders pulling tricks on a one-million-dollar aluminum vert ramp while freestyle motocross riders jumped over everything. I was good friends with Tony Hawk and the rest of the guys on the roster, and the tour turned out to be the most incredible six weeks of my life. The athletes were all so diverse that there was always something fun going on, whether it was taking each other's money gambling, going out to clubs at night, or just sitting on the bus driving from show to show.

Live bands played during every show, and one of them was Social Distortion—my favorite band of all time. Having them play while I rode was unreal. At some of the shows I was so focused on riding that I completely forgot about the 10,000 people sitting in the audience and just rode to push my own limits or to impress the other athletes sitting on the deck. I was pulling back-to-back double-tailwhips, no-handed 540-to-barspins, and 540-tailwhips straight into double-tailwhips, and it all felt incredible.

I had to miss a few contests during the 2002 season to go on the Huck Jam, but it was more than worth it. I remember sitting on the bus in between shows thinking, *Man I could stay on this tour for six months,* and it was completely true. I'm still planning to compete, but from now on, I'm taking every chance I get to go on a tour like that.

CONTEST MENTALITY

Contests have been mentally tough for me since day one. When you boil it down to the basics, a freestyle contest is just you against the ramps for seventy-five seconds straight. Every rider gets his allotted time, and it's up to him to pull his tricks in a way that sets him apart from the competition. Seventy-five seconds may not sound like much, but riding in a contest environment is a lot like running as fast as you can for that same amount of time. One crash can easily wreck a well-planned-out run, and your style and tricks have to be original if you want a top finish. Mix in a huge crowd, TV cameras, plus all the pressure you put on yourself, and contest days can wear you down pretty hard.

The way I treat contests now is a lot different than the way I used to. In 1996, instead of just dealing with the X Games as it happened, the contest haunted me for two months in advance. I would lie in bed every night thinking about how I wanted to ride and which tricks I wanted to do. When I

IT'S ALWAYS FUN TO SET STUFF UP ON STREET AND SEE WHAT YOU CAN DO. FAKIE WALLRIDE IN RALEIGH.

THIS BACKFLIP-TAILWHIP OVER A SPINE IN FRANCE WAS A DIRECT RESULT OF THE RESI SPINE IN MY WAREHOUSE.

went to the local skatepark, I would drill myself to get ready, doing tricks over and over to get them dialed.

After all the contests I've been in I've learned that I usually do my best when I have everything planned out ahead of time. I like to have a dialed run planned, where one trick leads into the next with minimal dead time in between. The more tricks flow together, the more "in the groove" I start to feel, and that can get me in the zone where everything works out. I also try to stay as calm as possible, which is easy to say but a lot harder to do. If a rider gets too excited he can start to tense up and flail around, but if he stays calm he can even recover from a mistake and easily move on to the next trick.

When it's time to go to a contest, every little thing adds up to the mental game. When practice starts, I try to fire big tricks right off the bat. For me, the slower I start out the tougher the contest is going to be, so I try to get things going right away. Plus, if there are multiple days of practice, going big on the first day gives me the confidence to keep riding at a higher level. Then when the contest starts, doing my hardest tricks doesn't feel as tough, since I've been firing them out for days. It's all a game of confidence, and the more prepared I feel, the more confident I become.

On the day of a contest, I always wake up early and eat a mellow breakfast. My mind is racing and butterflies are going crazy in my stomach. Once I start riding around, everything gets back into perspective. It may be a big contest, but it's still just me riding my bike, which is as fun today as it was when I started. The first part of a contest is qualifying, and only the top ten riders advance to the finals; that's where the big show begins.

When the finals start, I already have my two runs planned out and I feel pretty comfortable, but there's one thing you can never anticipate—the crowd. When 15,000 people are screaming while you ride it's the ultimate adrenaline rush. It can push you to pull incredible tricks, but it can also push you too far. I had heard loud audiences before, but when Vert was held indoors for the first time at the 2001 X Games in Philadelphia, the place went nuts. Hearing the crowd going off gave me a chill, and I had a lot of fun with the energy it created. It made me want to ride even better. Once I dropped in, though, my contest mentality took over. I blocked everything out and did what I needed to do for the win. In that mode, I focus on what needs to happen and then get it done.

Even after competing for more than ten years as a pro, contests can still throw me for a loop. I've learned that staying relaxed is the key, and hopefully after my first couple of airs, I'm at a place where I can be comfortable.

THE FUTURE

It's incredible to think that twenty-five years after first setting foot on a bike I'm still doing the same thing I was when I started: riding with my friends. I stay busy off my bike as well, and for the last two years I've even been involved in the Dave Mirra Celebrity Golf Tournament in Greenville, an event that raises money for charity. We've raised tens of thousands of dollars to benefit both the American Cancer Society and the Dream Factory, and that's something I plan to do for a long time.

As far as riding goes, I have no idea how long I will be able to keep going like I am now or how far I can push my limits. With the facilities that I have in the warehouse, the only thing that can hold me back is lack of ideas, and I keep coming up with new ones daily.

The reality is that I don't really plan my life too far into the future. Some people may think that's a mistake, but I'm still a rider, and that's not going to change for a long time. My bike has gotten me this far, and I'm sure it's got a lot more in store for me in the future.

WALL-TAP OFF A TEN-FOOT QUARTER AND OVER A SUB AT THE 2002 X GAMES. THIS WAS THE FIRST TIME IN A LONG TIME A WALLTAP SCARED ME.

MY FIVE FAVORITE CONTESTS

1. UGP ROOTS 2002. The Roots Jam is more of a grassroots contest, with no television cameras or businessmen. It's catered more to the hardcore street riders, which puts me in a weird position because I do ride in the X Games and the more commercialized events. This contest meant a lot to me because I put my emotions aside, rode my best, and ignored all the mixed vibes in the air. Despite the weird feelings, I ended up winning.

2. GRAVITY GAMES 2002, Street. The contest was a best-run-counts format, and I started out pretty weak in my first run. I came out for my second run and just went crazy. I didn't care if I won or lost. I just wanted to try a 720 over the spine, and I told myself that if I pulled it, I would link the hardest tricks I could do together, including a 180-tailwhip over the spine. I didn't even expect to win, but when they announced the results, I was in first.

3. GRAVITY GAMES 2000, Vert. I crashed really hard in practice. I hurt my calf pretty bad and got stitches near my eye. I was going to pull out of the contest, but then I sat back, thought about how long I'd worked to get that far, and decided I was not going to give up. I rode with no pressure or expectations. I won a gold medal for the vert contest, but in my eyes I got it for not giving up.

4. B.S. SERIES, DAYTONA BEACH, 1992. In the previous vert contest in London, England, I beat Mat Hoffman as a pro. That was the first professional vert contest Mat lost in more than three years, and there were some people saying they still thought Mat should have won. In Daytona, I rode perfectly and pulled a clean half-barspin–tailwhip, and to this day I've never pulled another in a vert contest. Not only was I the first to beat Mat Hoffman, but I beat him in two contests in a row when I was seventeen years old, my rookie year as a pro.

5. AFA MASTERS, COLUMBUS, OHIO, FLATLAND, 1987. This was my first national contest ever, and all the riders I read about in the magazines were there. At the time I was cosponsored by Haro Bikes. I met Dennis McCoy, my all-time-favorite rider at the contest, and got to ride with him. When it was time for my run, I was so nervous that I touched, stumbled, and fell through it. I cried afterward because I was so disappointed. I ended up finishing eleventh place out of twelve riders. I went home and rode harder than ever and prepared for the next contest, which was only a few months away. That contest really taught me a lesson to try my best and never give up.

POSING FOR ANOTHER FOX AD ON THE TOUR.
CHECK OUT THE NEON LIGHT.

PROPERTY LINE
CTLY ENFORCED

 I ALSO, AND I ARE PUTTING A LOT OF WORK INTO MY NEW WEB SITE, DAVEMIRRA.COM. IT'S COOL GIVING KIDS A GLIMPSE OF WHAT GOES ON IN MY LIFE ON A DAILY BASIS.

ONE HAPPY TWENTY-*FIVE*-YEAR OLD.

ACKNOWL

EDGMENTS

ACKNOWLEDGMENTS

I WOULD LIKE TO THANK GOD, MOM, DAD, MY BROTHER TIM, MY FAMILY, MY FRIENDS, STEVE ASTEPHEN, GARY REAM, DENNIS MCCOY, MARK EATON, KEVIN JONES AND THE PLYWOOD HOODS, WOODY ITSON, TONY D., JIM FORD, MAT HOFFMAN, JIM COOK, KAREN RALSTON, JIM BROWN, GENE WAGNER, LINDY'S BIKE LOFT, FRED BLOOD, WAYNE'S BIKE SHOP, RON WILKERSON, DINO DELUCA, BRIAN BLYTHER, DAVE NOURIE, JENNY J., SIMBA, J.J., PRINCESS, AND MELLY FOR ALL THE INSPIRATION AND CONTINUOUS SUPPORT THEY HAVE PROVIDED FOR ME AND THE PATH I CHOSE.

PHOTO CREDITS

Photo credits:

Brad McDonald/*Ride BMX*: i, iv–v, x–1, 44–45, 48–49, 58–59, 64–65, 70–71, 94–95, 97, 136–137; Mark Losey/*Ride BMX*: ii–iii, vi–vii, 32–33, 60–61, 74–75, 82–83, 84–85, 88–89, 104–105, 106, 107, 108, 110–111, 117, 120–121, 122–123, 126–127, 128–129, 131, 134–135, 140–141, 142–143, 146–147, 154–155, 166, 168, 172, 173, 174–175, 177 (both), 178, 180–181, 182–183, 185, 186; Mark Losey/*BMX Plus!*: 54–55, 66–67, 96; courtesy of the Mirra family: viii–ix, 2–3, 4, 5, 8–9, 10, 12, 18–19, 20–21, 23, 26–27, 30–31, 34–35, 36–37, 62–63, 72–73, 76–77, 80–81; Steve Buddendeck/Axis: 6–7, 50–51, 53, 68–69, 86–87, 90–91, 98–99, 103, 113, 124, 130; Jim Cook: 13, 14–15; Mike Blabac/DC Shoes: 16–17; Trevor Graves: 24–25, 28–29; Tarrick: 38–39, 42–43; Adam Booth/*BMX Plus!*: 40–41, 46–47, 114, 119, 165 (right), 184; Pete Demos/Haro Bikes: 56–57, 146–147; Haro Bikes: 78–79, 92–93, 116, 138–139, 148–149; Fox Racing: 102; Mike Laird: 115, 118; Road Champs: 125; Markus Paulsen: 132–133; Carl Hyndman/DC Shoes: 150–151, 156–157, 160–161, 162–163, 164 (left), 170–171; Jeff "Boomer" Alred: 152–153, 160, 161, 164–165 (middle), 167, 169.